Living the River

Kate Tongs

Living the River

Acknowledgements

'Childhood Memories', 'Childhood', 'Kayaking on the lake', 'Old Man Oak', 'The antique chair', 'Visiting Nanna' were previously published in *The Persistence of Song*, 2013
'Childhood', 'Love is' and 'Visiting Nanna' in *Word Weavers*, 2010
'Inspiration' in *Poet's Republic,* 2010
'Recipe for a rainbow' in *The Mozzie,* 2012
and *Valley Micropress,* 2012
'The Beach' in *The Mozzie,* 2011
'River Romance' in *Poetry D'Amour,* 2017)
'Walking the Pipeline Track', 'Visiting Nanna' and 'The cool man fern' in *Falling into Birdsong,* 2015
'Love is' in *Poet's Republic,* 2008

Thank you to my family and to my poetry colleagues,
especially to Liz Winfield for her guidance and assistance,
and to Robyn Mathison for her ongoing encouragement.

Dedicated to my family and friends

Living the River
ISBN 978 1 76109 337 1
Copyright © Kate Tongs 2022

First published 2022 by
Ginninderra Press
PO Box 3461 Port Adelaide 5015
www.ginninderrapress.com.au

Contents

Another beautiful day	7
To live is…	8
Childhood memories	9
The poppy paddock	10
Bathtime at the Springs	11
Childhood	12
Apricots on a green table	13
The ideal	14
Yacht on a winter's morning	15
How to paint emotions	16
Petra	17
When shadows fall	18
Escher's share house	19
Lost and found	20
The unruly handbag	21
Sphinx Rock dreaming	22
Inspiration	23
Stopping for a photograph	24
Spring's nectar	25
To the moon	26
The ice-cave	27
My love	28
Groom and bride	29
Birds of prey	30
Moments	31
Defining features	32
The photograph	33
My lamb	34
Recipe for a rainbow	35
The forest angel	36

Morning by the water	37
The beach	38
Things that make my soul sing	40
Elemental	41
The young gardener	42
River romance	43
Stitching	44
Departure	45
Homeward path	46
Kayaking on the lake	47
Leaving my lover	48
Old Man Oak	49
Stand strong	50
Walking the Pipeline Track	51
The antique chair	52
The Mulberry	53
In the moment – a found poem – from *Breathe* magazine	54
Night's ink	55
Tip shop	56
On the veranda	58
Love is	59
Atlas café	60
An ordinary morning	61
Found Poem after Elizabeth Bard's *Lunch in Paris*	63
Visiting Nanna	64
What I learned from my father	66
The cool man fern	67

Another beautiful day

Waist wrapped
with wreath of kelp
she combs the wrack
for tidal treasures.
Part-filled with sand
an amber cone-shell
sounds low in the breeze.
Glinting green, glowing glass,
softened by surf and sand.
And dried weed,
        worn wood,
                smooth stone.
She picks them up.
Puts them down.
The girl smiles shyly,
lowers her eyes.
The sun greets her gently
from an autumn horizon.

To live is…

To dream
and sing a song by candlelight.

To breathe the cool and salty air
and feel the crunch of grainy sand.

To touch the water and the wind,
row a boat beneath the moon
and sail a starlit sky.

To climb a mountain topped with white
and dip your toe in an icy stream.

Extend your hand to someone else
and whisper thank you as a prayer.

Childhood memories

Effervescent sunshine
pours through
torrential rainclouds.

Grandpa drives
a dust-laden tractor
over open grassy paddocks,
while eastern rosellas
feast on hawthorn berries.

Floods levels rise
by the red-brick flour mill.
Falling-down sheds
are strewn with rusty machinery.

Polwarth rams
with rolling fleece
butt their heads.

Black-feathered chooks
lay golden eggs.

Fat milking cow
drags a full udder.
Dozens of cats
wait for her milk.

Yellow skivvies and sunflowers.
Daddy sings
on his way
to the cowshed.

The poppy paddock

Windswept children
with freckled noses
and iridescent smiles
stand tall in a field
of opium poppies.
Blue shirts surrounded
by deep mauve blooms
soon to form dusky grey heads
dripping with alkaloids.
Innocents playing
before a harvest.
Flowers of peace,
flowers of power.

Bathtime at the Springs

Visiting Sarah's farmhouse on the coast
I like to bathe in pastel coloured bathroom.
A deep cast-iron, claw-footed tub
stands waiting in the room
brimming with bubbles
shrouded by a white curtain:
shower rail, head height.
Old brass-handled taps
jut out from the smooth tiled wall
and a pale blue bathmat
adorns the wooden floor.
In the corner is an old sink
and beside it sits a fern.
Looking out the window
I see lambs grazing on a green field.
The walls of the room are painted yellow
and gently peeling away.
I hang my dressing gown
on the hook behind the door,
immerse my body in the warm water
and drift across the ocean.

Childhood

Climbing through tart, purple mulberries
Warm, frothy, sweet-scented milk
Bobbing, golden daffodils
Pebbly, leafy fairy gardens
Melodic splash of an oar in gently flowing river
Wild black swan fluttering her wings
Nailing boards for cubbies in pungent pines
Hooking the first slimy flathead in the bay
Moulding smoky sand volcanoes at Pelican Point
Shrill cooees across the valley
Diving into a cold stream at Easter
Skipping swiftly to an old song
Dressing cuddly kittens in knitted dolls' clothes
Striking a harmonic chord on the burly antique piano
Riding a bicycle with no hands
Curling up on the corner of the couch
Nibbling on golden ginger biscuits
Reading by torchlight under bedclothes
Falling asleep fulfilled at end of day

Apricots on a green table

Mum is on a mission to preserve fruit. The storeroom cupboard is already lined with tomatoes peaches and pears. Brow furrowed, she pares apricots slicing swiftly through succulent amber flesh. The green Laminex tabletop is awash with juice. Digging in the sharp point of the red-handled knife, she removes a blemish and flicks out the kernel – smooth and round like a small stone. The curved halves are pushed to the bottom of a glass Fowler's jar which stands on the edge of the sink. Through the kitchen window she views a blue wren resting briefly, head tilted to one side as he inspects. When the jar is full, Mum pours in sugar water from a stainless-steel jug till it reaches the brim. Every now and then she pauses to wipe her hands on her home-made apron. A plastic bowl sits on the tabletop for stones and scraps which the chooks will feast on shortly. The potent aroma of ripe apricots penetrates the air. It is warm. Mum wipes her face. She works ceaselessly, filling each jar, pulling a thick rubber band onto its rim and placing a tin lid on its top. Eight jars are placed in the boiler, which is half filled with water. Soon we will eat them with crumble and fresh cream for dessert.

The ideal

Barefoot she tends her vegetable patch
long, blonde hair blowing in the breeze.
Her ankle-length floral dress
is worn and patched.

She gazes out to the point.
Her wild-eyed lover is on his board again,
bronzed shoulders supple
as he paddles out towards the next set.

She pulls a weed,
her hands cracked and earthy,
and digs in the fork,
harvests beets and potatoes
to roast for the evening meal.

The sun glows low over the hills
and an inky darkness creeps in.
The moon rises
and the ocean turns to silver.

Yacht on a winter's morning

Your sleek body beckons
from seat of ice-blue sea.

A triangle of mast and stays
thrusts over the horizon
to greet the waking sun.
Bowline angles to amber buoy.

White hull ripples
shimmer on the water.
Tide turns the tiller.

In the voiceless day
Captain strokes his
bearded chin.
Cat curls on cabin cushion.
Shelters from the morning chill.

You sway a little in the swell
and creak and groan with cold.
Immersed in conversation
with birds and breeze.

How to paint emotions

Passion is
the deep purple rose
of a dark rich chocolate

Heartbreak is
a bird
with a broken wing
resting
on a crack in the ice sheet

Anger is
the fist held tight
in a blood-red carcass

Fear is
a lone boy in the dark
sensing
a striking snake

Happiness is
the brightly coloured rainbow
of a child's sure smile.

Petra

I can still see you standing
in a red cathedral
carved into the cliff face
in the ancient city.

Pillars face canyoned streets
and our song resounds
on stone walls
as we sing 'Amazing Grace'
with grace.

The shadows extend
and a handful of tourists
in shorts and T-shirts
clap their hands.

We are interrupted
by the soar of smoking jet-fighters
which roar over us
in a chase above the ruins.

The heat fades
and the sounds cease.
There is a chill
in the still air
and footprints in the sand.

When shadows fall

Reality passes slowly
when the sun burns
low on the horizon
and shadows fall.

Stars glow
like catseyes
through midnight blue.

You bear my weight
as I lean against
your wiry body.

Like a time-traveller's wife
I hold you close
in the moment
lest you slip away.

Escher's share house

(or In disarray)

I am a dwarf
in a cave
on a cloud
hanging by a thread
distended from the light bulb.

What mountain is this?
I ask of an ant-hill
Standing in the stairwell.

The chandelier projects
upwards from the floor.
Its crystal shards a dangerous sculpture.

A giant brown eye
gazes in
criss-crossed by wooden window frame –

disappears
in a puff of smoke
streaming from the upside-down chimney.

Lost and found

A lost bird
on the limb
of the tree of my mind
sings of broken dreams.

A still small voice
finds its way to my heart, knowing
I breathe the here and now.

The unruly handbag

The handbag contains a dotty umbrella
A stolen blue biro
        fast running out of ink
A small blue diary with numerous scribbled entries
        flowers for Christine
        visit Aunt Jan
Some floral perfume in a glass bottle
        seeping with roses
An android smart phone in a red leather case
        buzzing like a busy bee
Various credit cards, ID and a bus pass
        worn through over use
A small green purse covered in Irish wildflowers
        carrying coins for parking and coffees
A dog-eared family photo
Various tissues and screwed up bits of paper
A small hairbrush entangled with grey-brown strands
Some old lipstick, a moisturising sunblock
        and the odd dust bunny
Reaching in for the phone is a lucky dip
And in a desperate search for house keys,
the contents are frequently spewed on the front steps.

Sphinx Rock dreaming

Legs dangling
over the sheer drop
you laugh
and incline your head
towards the Organ Pipes
as I watch over
leafless ghost-gums,
their white trunks
extending up to meet us
on Sphinx Rock.
I dream of flying
down from my dolerite seat
to the mossy forest floor below.
You look upwards
at the mountain's rugged face
basking in the cool-blue sky beyond.

Inspiration

Inspiration is our friend.
We chase him on, though worlds may end.
And inspiration shows his face.
Through calm surrounds
he alters pace.
And through anachronistic leaps
appears above the morbid sounds
of trains and cars and dreary towns.
He smiles on souls with greater dreams
than mortgage, rent and work in teams.
Above the grey and dull cements
he tiptoes though the world laments,
then leaps and soars and glides and bounds.
His smile is seen, his soul is found.
He's in the garden, bright and lush.
A hand of cards. A royal flush.
A dewdrop glistening in the sun.
A house of games. A land of fun.
We chase him on through rain and hail,
while lesser beings, drawn and pale,
recede and let him flee.

Stopping for a photograph

Wind waves its way through broad- leafed trees
and ferrous soil shines bright.
I make my way by sandy track
to sparkling sea and dancing light

Spring's nectar

The clematis hums with bees,
pale-yellow anthers, pollen-laden,
white petals peering at the sun.

It creeps along the deck,
warming slowly through
the nectar-filled air.

Drones dance in circles,
and vibrate their tiny wings,
collecting food for their siblings,
who hatch in honeycomb.

To the moon

Let's drink our wine by moonlight
beneath the silver smile
of Earth's ever faithful satellite
on evening calm and mild.

And when our view is clouded
and we cannot see the way
the moon it seems is shrouded
in a veil of lightish grey.

Remaining always good and true
with your hue of yellow-white
to the moon I say 'I'll toast you'
just the two of us tonight.

The ice-cave

I draw breath
sharply
in the cold,
beneath the glinting sun.

Crampons gripping ice shelf,
step by slow step
I make my way towards you
across a solid white sheet.

In a cool-blue ice cave,
you meet my gaze,
breathe the frozen air
of the glacier.

I am afraid to smile
lest the ice melts,
extend my gloved hand
into your firm grasp.

You lead me through
the heart-shaped exit.
I draw breath safely
in the world beyond.

My love

You are a daisy in the lawn
dripping with dew.

You are a sunflower
face tilted towards the sun.

You are a river red-gum
sturdy and sound.

You are an open green orchid
virile and fresh.

Groom and bride

See the bride
swollen with child
extend her hand

See the groom
full of pride
one good man

Side by side
arm in arm
groom and bride

Birds of prey

Here I perch
high in my eyrie
extending my wings.
Small birds shy away
as my keen eyes
search the sky.
The sun sinks low.
You return and hover
with your broad reach,
talons clasping limp carcass.
You land beside me
and we feast on warm flesh.
You sit beside your eager young,
ever watchful.

Moments

I remember the day Mum arrived home
with my red-faced baby brother,
I balanced a bike on two wheels and proudly rode past Dad.

I used to skip on the netball court during lunch break,
would dive into a pool from a plank on a willow bough
and learnt to drive in a rusty run-down old Ford
with my friend in the front paddock.

One Christmas I was given a shy Burmese kitten,
It hid in the doll's house
and had to be coaxed out with cream.

When I was 18, I ran away to Nepal.
I can still see the mountains
glowing in the half-light of dusk.

I remember standing up on a surf board
and riding a party wave
at Clifton beach, with Sally and Rick.
I fell in laughing.

And floating over a fragile sponge garden
deep beneath the sea.

Eating breakfast on the balcony
and viewing a golden sun rise over distant hills.

But my greatest thrill was when you took my hand,
and held our new baby close to my heart.

Defining features

On the tip of my finger
is a scar from the knife.
Slicing cheddar as a child
I bled blood-orange red.

High up on my right inner thigh
is a heart-shaped mark.
A splash of rouge
I've had since birth.

The left side of my mouth
bears a single dimple
that crinkles when I laugh.
My smile is warm.

In the small of my back
lies a surgeon's scar
angry and raised.
Memento mori.

The photograph

Mum looks angelic.
She sits, face soft and hair silver white,
nursing a motherless lamb,
wrapped in star-covered blanket.

My son, aged five,
stands beside her,
wriggles in his boots,
and waits to feed the lamb
warm milk from a rubber teat.

Behind them fresh flowers
sit on an antique bookcase,
resting on polished floorboards
and a worn Persian rug.

The photo was taken in the living room
on the first day of spring.
I put it in an envelope
and post it home for Father's Day.

My lamb

It's leaving you behind that breaks my heart:
>your arms outstretched
>your pleading eyes
>your tears.

Recipe for a rainbow

Place seven crystals
in a large golden croc.
Mix with raindrops.
Break in a cloud.
Stir on a still day.
Heat with a pinch of sunlight,
by an ocean vista,
for an instant,
and say voila!
Choose a child
as a witness.

The forest angel

Through tall myrtle, beds of ferns and mossy floor
he treads lightly on the earth,
carrying smoked tofu, fresh berries and yoghurt
to the girl in her eyrie
who protects the trees.

He brings a bucket of water,
cold as snowmelt,
for her daily baptism
and greets her warmly
above the calling birds.

She smiles a gentle smile,
spreads her lacy wings
and flies down to meet him.

Morning by the water

An amber sun
lights the sky
reflecting in ripples
as the water licks the shore.

In the shallows
a small boy in a wet-suit
clings to his boogie board
shrieking with joy
as his eager parents
guide him in with the waves.

A man moves swiftly
towards a large dark diamond shape
and splashes to fend off
an inquisitive sting ray.

Horseshoe jellies
wobble in the wrack-line
adorned with weed and shells.

On her homeward leg
a jogger pauses and pants
stops still in the sand
mesmerised by the morning sun.

The beach

Sun-browned bodies
beneath the glaring sun
lunging and thrusting
over volleyball nets.

Plump middle-aged mums
glowing pink cheeked
beneath their
broad-brimmed
straw hats.

Freckled noses
covered in zinc cream
playing tippedy
with their brothers.

Drenched ponytails
on pretty girls
of ten and twelve
skinny-legged like seabirds
in the lapping waves.

Moulded sandcastles
with stick soldiers
surrounded by moats.

Shaggy dogs
shaking their wet
sandy fur
furiously.

Friendly sea breeze
gently easing
the heat of the day.

Things that make my soul sing

An arrow arcing cleanly through the crisp, cool air
An oar gently splashing on a deep, still lake
A dew-laden fern curling downwards from its tip
A snow-capped summit pushing through a cloud-laden sky
A wheel turning swiftly on a bicycle track
A wave lapping lyrically on the bow of a boat
A full blue moon shining brightly in the night
My faithful old hound curled warmly on my lap
A cosy fire crackling and sending up sparks
A cat's eyes glowing golden-green in the dark

Elemental

Air:
Clear blue-grey and white
Embrace the breeze, whirling wind
Blown away by an unknown spirit

Fire:
Crimson, green and gold
Searing heat, heart-felt passion
Lick the flickering flames of our wild lovemaking

Earth:
Warm chocolate clay clods
Footprinted pathway overland
Birthplace of your seed – sodden in the dew

Water:
Soothing aqua-green
Deep pools of emotion well over
Forever waving you farewell

The young gardener

His boots
are dark-tanned leather
and sturdy as a thoroughbred

His fore arms
are rippled muscle
and eager as a new bull.

He hands me
an amber pumpkin,
plump as a breastfed babe.

His smile is
wide-eyed innocence
and sweet as honeydew melon.

River romance

The dinghy is old timber, peeling paint and leaking fast.
You row me slowly.
And as I bail, your brow furled deeply,
you feed me on philosophy.
A black swan curves her slender neck
and wood duck chase across the lake.
The bank, overhanging with blackberries
beckons us share a sweet, tart treat.
Paddles plip plop and drip.
You draw them backwards through the air.
The boat, as my heart, has wings.
Red rowlocks creak and turn in rhythm.
And I, still bailing, smiling,
hear the soft spring breeze whisper
as your fingers twist through my tousled hair
and the back of your hand
gently brushes my cheek.

Stitching

I sit and stitch.
Rose-scented
soft melodies
drift through the air.

Mending my woollen top
my memory shifts to times
when the roses were fresh
from my mother's garden.

Bright red and white
they bloom forever in my mind
till their petals wilt
and blow away in the wind.

By a vase on the mantel
I see Mum now:
sitting, stitching.

Departure

As you walk away
a thin ribbon of light
snakes its way over the hills.

I sit in the silence of tall trees
watching
as distant waves crash in.

I am left
with the emptiness
of dark night.

Homeward path

Follow the narrow highway which curls around the coast.
Go inland beyond deep mauve hills
into a grassy valley plateau
where the little Swan River flows
past an old kirk with arched windows and open door.
Turn off at a weatherboard cellar door
along a gravel road lined with hawthorn
over a cattle-grid and past a mob of shorn sheep.
Pass a wooden hay shed with rusty corrugated roof
and a silo that smells of freshly harvested grain.
Come to an unruly pine hedge
and up the drive to a yellow-painted Georgian homestead
with shady veranda and winding wisteria.
There you will find me on the rocking chair
sleeping in the warmth of the afternoon sun.

Kayaking on the lake

Swans arch their graceful necks
and swim in circles of courtship.
Ducks flutter feathers
and extend beaks for bread.
We launch from the lakeside –
surface glistening gold
in the setting sun,
paddles dripping in clear water.
Edging our way across
we speak in whispers.
The rising moon
shines over us
a silvery glow.
I feel my boat beneath me,
smooth and streamlined,
gliding over the ripples.
The night is still.
We slide into a narrow damp canyon,
moss-lined walls alight with glow-worms.
We sit and watch a while,
then slowly, silently
paddle home.

Leaving my lover

It was a dewy night.
I murmured a prayer,
rolled over
and fell into slumber.

Beneath soft down
and crisp linen
I drifted quietly into dreamland
in the arms of my lover.

He felt me shudder in the night,
rolled over
and fell into slumber.

Waking with me cold
and rigid in his arms.
It was a breezy morning.

I watched his silent tears
roll slowly from brown eyes
and float away.

Old Man Oak

Old man oak,
a weathered English face
in an Australian farmland,
looks out from his mane of leaves,
fluorescent green
against a blue sky,
oval shaped
with extended, short,
finger-like projections
and branched venation.
Body covered
in thick, furrowed,
grey-brown bark –
his armour
against an army of insects.
Birds nest in tangled branches
and acorns spring to life
in the rich soil at his feet.
Children and possums
climb like monkeys
along his long limbs.
He bears a wrinkled smile
on his wooden face
as if to say
'They're in my care.'

Stand strong

I seize the morning light,
the chorusing birds
and step out into a new day.

A pademelon
grazing the neighbour's garden
looks up
pounds the earth as it bounds away.

I wonder how it feels
to steal grass from stolen land.

I increase my gait
and view the mountain
in its morning glow.

Kunanyi stands tall,
defies the sprawling city
with stiff dolerite face.

Whispering to the wind
I came first,
and I stand strong.

Walking the Pipeline Track

Rhododendrons overflow from the park,
tall trees overhang the path.
We walk briskly through the ferns,
sturdy old men with embracing arms.
I step under an old pipeline as gurgling,
babbling water runs away down the mountainside.
We stop briefly to quench our thirst,
hands cupped in the cold stream.
I hear the plop of a coin in St Crispin's Well
as you make a secret wish.
We stretch our muscles and pant up a slope,
then rest at the foot of Silver Falls.
We listen to the flow of the lyrical water
and the music of the birds,
then return to the café
to share a slice of Hummingbird cake.

The antique chair

Great-great Aunt Trix
sits in the corner of the room,
curved, walnut-coloured back
inclined slightly
to face the sun,
cushioned body
missing a few springs.
Her cream skirt
embroidered with crewel birds.
from a generation past.
The old spinster
peers through the window
of the stone house
on the knoll,
spying on the neighbours,
waiting for her soldier,
bearing the weight
of a fat cat
purring on her lap.

The Mulberry

As a child
I climbed your sloping branches
adhered to rough bark
unafraid of falling
head obscured by leaves.
I feasted
crimson-stained lips and fingers
told the tale.
I carried a bucket
half-full
of treats
that somehow never
reached the brim.

In the moment – a found poem – from *Breathe* magazine

Dreamy, ephemeral, playful
the turning of the tide
has its pull.
Childlike happy once more
dipping your toes
to wash your worries away.
Whisk you through the whimsical world
on those frosty mornings
of a winter's delight.
Completely in the moment
dancing on the waves.

Night's ink

In night's ink
the air chills
shrilly.
Wild tree-shadows
are dancing madmen
menacing murder
on dark paths.
Gusts batter
a lone walker
shoulders shrugged
against the wind.
Ice burns
and Antarctic blasts
wrack his frame.
Mauve lips drawn
against the cold,
frozen fingers
clasp keys.
With hollow steps
the man plods home
and somehow safely
finds the light.

Tip shop

Second Chance Re-Use
Bold green words
boast opportunity.
Treasures greet you
by the door:
        stained teacups
        worn leather boots
leftover curtains.
A faded red dress hangs limply on a rack.
Kitchenware is half-price today.
25 cent plates pile high.
Shelves house dusty glasses
        and a dented metal bowl.
A wonky-eyed china doll in need of love
sits by fluffy dog with bursting seams.
A fire poker menaces
a broken-stringed guitar.
Discarded saws hang – jaws open
        over an old tandem.
There are rows of yellowed books:
        How to pick a racehorse
        Treasure Island
and old movies.
Abandoned art adorns the walls:
        green and yellow boathouses
        a red and blue lorikeet.

Dampness permeates the air.
The smell of mould is everywhere.
Among the brown lamp shades
odd golf clubs
rusty bikes and
chairs missing springs,
I finally find
that dodgy blender
I always needed.

On the veranda

In cane chair she sits,
weathered brow
deep in daydreams.

She is brown and plump
as her childhood pony.
Life has been kind.

A bantam fluffs her feathers.
She twists a coil of hair
as it floats down her face.

By her feet a child
plays with pebbles,
tugs at her sleeve.

By her side, eyes half-open,
a ginger cat twitches
and stretches out of slumber.

Her ample husband,
hand on belly,
slowly sips his sugary tea.

Love is

A fish flashing past in the ocean
A merry-go-round by the seaside
An ice cream melting in the summer sun
The softest breeze on the hottest day of the year
Autumn leaves gently falling to the ground
An amber sunset at the end of a long day
A roaring fire on a cool evening
A million diamonds in the night sky
A cup of fresh black tea in the morning
A homespun cardigan that keeps you warm in winter
The sweet scent of jasmine flowering
A couple ambling along a country road
The bleating of a newborn lamb in spring
A child's tight-fisted grip

Atlas café

'You're beautiful'
announces the sign
at the coffee shop door.
At 9 a.m. the queue stretches
into the street.

I stand in line
admiring walls papered with maps
of far-off places
that take me into their dreams.

The fridge is stocked with
bircher muesli and fruit salad.
I choose a vegan bliss ball

and offer my cup
for a chai latte
completing a paper bag survey
Are you a hugger?
as I wait
not indiscriminately.

An ordinary morning

Awaking from a dream
I rise to a new dawn
listen to the gush of the heat pump
and feel its warm breath against my legs
as I pass by.

Sitting still in the corner chair,
I breathe
        out and in
        in and out
through alternate nostrils
for five mindful minutes.

The velvet aroma
of ground coffee
permeates the air
slowly sipped

I fry a breakfast egg
for my son
and watch him eat.

I make my husband a sandwich
Fresh bread
spread with home-made chutney
cheese and ham.

I usher my son
to shower and dress for school.
help him tie his laces
and add his drink bottle
to the side pocket
of his unruly school bag.

The clock chimes eight times.

Found Poem after Elizabeth Bard's *Lunch in Paris*

The hens bolted forward
A set of cathedral-sized doors heaved open
blanketing the streets in silent white

I open an old clothes hamper filled with tutus
Rehearsing for a full-scale musical comedy
There were neither undershirts nor geraniums
It smelled as if it might rain cinnamon

Add the olive oil, shallots, garlic and orange zest
Just a skinny guy, stark raving naked, smoking a cigarette
Almost every woman from sixteen to sixty, wearing a bikini

Escargots: each iridescent shell filled
with pungent green paste of parsley and garlic butter
Women who pick at their food hate sex

After the fairy tale
she kissed me on both cheeks –
a willowy brunette with a few scattered freckles
on a woven plastic chair
wedged behind a small table
Sipping her café

Statues of scientists and philosophers line the balconies
Mother, in her grey cashmere coat, in hot pursuit
expensive sunglasses perched on top of her head

The promised land doesn't quite exist
But we are getting there.

Visiting Nanna

joyfully I fill
stained china
with black tea
listen to the hum
and rattle of the wheel
spinning
rhythmically
whirring
wool turning
from greasy fleece
into fine thread
Nanna pauses
board game in play
'nice' I spell
'id'
Nanna triple word scores
and wins
by a fraction
tasty cheese
on dry crackers
the cat purrs
and raises her half tail
Nanna's face creases
as she smiles
and talks
of days gone by
glamorous days
when she played piano
and wore
her fine black hair

in a tousled bun
now grey and curled short
she rests
in velvet covered arm chair
listens
as I repent my sins
and smiles again
tells of days
she rode a motorbike
and turned down
a diamond ring
for a full life
of country comforts
and seven children
she milked cows
attended church
lived and loved
joyfully I fill
stained china
with black tea

What I learned from my father

My father taught me
>that a giant can be gentle
>and dwarves deserve respect
>and nothing is worth more than a true heart.

He taught me that circumstance
>can shape a soul
>and there is a gem in every mineshaft.

He told me if I extend my hand
>to anyone in need
>there will always be a white flag.

My father taught me
in an open meadow with many flowers:
>Life is an adventure,
a dance of delight.

The cool man fern

(for Jeff)

You are:
the strength of the oak tree
a well-chiselled statue
the cool man fern
a supple fig branch
the refreshing fountain
the soft green lawn
a calling wattlebird
a gentle willow
the open gate
the well-trodden path
a warm smooth stone.
You are my love.

www.ingramcontent.com/pod-product-compliance
Lightning Source LLC
Chambersburg PA
CBHW070337120526
44590CB00017B/2917